A Gloomorous Book In Verse

George Genovese

A Gloomorous Book In Verse

For Mum, Dad
and my three great brothers – Mario, John and Chris

Thank you to Meia Geddes in appreciation
of her valuable suggestions

A Gloomorous Book In Verse
ISBN 978 1 76041 810 6
Copyright © text George Genovese 2019
Cover artwork: Chris Genovese

First published 2019 by
GINNINDERRA PRESS
PO Box 3461 Port Adelaide 5015 Australia
www.ginninderrapress.com.au

Contents

Warning!	9
Alphabet Song	10
Hare Higgs	11
I Have a Funny Nose	13
Bright Mister Pee	14
Animal Alphabet	15
Old Gobbledegook	18
The Clever Frog	19
The Thin Boy	21
Naughty Fun	22
Siggy Calf	23
New-age Witch	24
The Squawkle	26
The Hole	30
Unfinished poem	32
The Mad Queen of Nullyannay	33
The Gorilla	37
The Dodo	38
The Skunk	39
The Weasel	40
The Chameleon	41
The Squirrel	42
The Lyrebird	43
The Turkey	44
The Goat	45
The Comb Duck	46
Tommy Toucan	47
The Bean-man	55
Shorty and Stretch	57
Limericks	67

Unhappy Ted	69
The End of the Road	75

Awl characters inn this book are factitious and any dissemblance too persons, places, concepts oar things, living, dead, oar somewhere between, is purely fundamental. Accept four the purpose of research, private study, criticism oar review, know part of this book may bee reproduced oar transmitted buy any means, electronic, mechanical, photographic oar telepathic, without the written emission of the punisher and is otherwise a breech of copywrite and perishable buy lore.

Awl writes deserved © 3019

Warning!

Oh no! You've opened up the book,
I hope you don't regret it,
for if you'd rather not have fun
you better just forget it!

I warn you, if some silliness
brings on unwelcome laughter,
well, let's just get it over now –
this book's not what you're after.

If you're not one for craziness
and language weird and punning,
then I suggest, make like a nose
and blow or just get running.

Unless you're fondly looking for
absurdly rolling verses,
it'll strike you as amusing as
ten badly driven hearses.

Don't feel obliged but put it down
if ours a differing humour,
I'll lose a sale but that's all right,
I'll keep my sense of gloomour.

Look, go and find some other book,
there's many a good one near,
if I may say, you can't go wrong
with Tolkien, Dahl or Lear.

Alphabet Song

Before I sang
my A B C,
do you suppose
that we were we?
My D E F
and G H I,
was Geoff my name
and I still I?
Before I learnt
my J K L,
what I believed
I cannot tell,
my M N O
and P Q R,
that time now seems
so very far.
Before I said
my S T U
was I as speechless
as a shoe?
V W X
and Y and Zed,
were all these questions
in my head?

Hare Higgs

Yes, words can so puzzle,
befuddle and seem
as crazy and muddled
as a fuzzy old dream.

Take the hare who's no hair
and known as Hare Higgs,
so fluffy with hair
he's scornful of wigs!

Just note his short tail
and note you this too,
he's short of a tale
that he could tell you.

With such a cute nose
that knows very well,
it knows not a little
how noses might smell.

With long slender ears
and corns on his feet,
but no juicy ears
of corn he can eat.

Oh how he loves carrots
all crispy and cold,
but holds no affection
for carats of gold.

He'll nibble an eggplant
which no way deceives,
the chickens make eggs
and never the trees!

He loves to get lettuce
from far away friends,
but not the dry letters
you scribble with pens.

And nibbling the thyme
he steals from your plot,
he'll watch all the time
though no watch has he got.

He'll munch a dressed salad
by shady gazebos,
but hates the idea
of leeks in tuxedos!

And while he might wonder
while hopping the croft,
why his soles are so hard
when his soul is so soft;

he somehow believes
in spite of men's chatter,
as long as he's happy,
well then, there's no matter!

I Have a Funny Nose

I have a funny nose
and so has Daddy too,
and when our noses blow
it's like a big wind blew.

I have a funny nose
and so has Mummy too,
and when our noses flow
it's like some sticky glue.

I have a funny nose
and so has doggy too,
and when we both have colds
our noses go, 'Ah-choo!'

Yes, in our funny family
there's not a serious nose,
they run, run in our family,
like a dripping hose.

Bright Mister Pee

'Oh deary me,' said Mister Pee,
'my one good sock is damp,
and when I put my foot inside
it gives me an awful cramp!

Oh deary me, I'm due for tea,
so what am I to do?
I wish I had another sock
that won't turn my toes blue.

Aha!' he said. 'I'll use my head,
I know what I'm about!
I'll shift the dampness from inside
by turning it inside out!

And then the damp won't give me cramp
but rub my shoe instead,
there's never cause for fuss or fret
when you just use your head!'

So Mister Pee went, 'One, two, three,
now there the job is done!
I'll try it on and maybe I
can go and have some fun.'

But Mister Pee said, 'Deary me,
the damp is here to stay!'
Still, he liked his idea so much
he wore that sock all day!

Animal Alphabet

A is for aardvark
who eats a white-ant,
B is for blackbird
no friend of the bat,

C is for cougar
a kind of big cat,
D is for doggy
who likes a good pat,

E is for eagle
who glides in the sky,
F is for falcon
who's gliding as high,

G is for goldfish
who swims in the lake,
H is for hippo
who's still not awake,

I is for ibis
who catches a fish,
J is for jackal
and meat is his dish,

K is for kea
who sings all the spring,
L is for lion
who'll roar but not sing,

M is for monkey,
a cheeky old chap,
N is for nuthatch
who'll have none of that,

O is for orca
who's swimming the deep,
P is for panda
who'd rather just sleep,

Q is for quetzal
a colourful bird,
R is for reindeer
who lives in a herd,

S is for spider
who catches a fly,
T is for tiger
who doesn't know why,

U is for upapa,
a beautiful bird,
V is for vulture
who's always alert,

W's for walrus
who mourns a lost home,
X is extinct,*
so x is unknown,

Y is for yeti**
who's not seen a trap,
Z is for zebra
who says, 'Lucky chap!

The rest of us creatures
have suffered in traps,
have lost our poor lives
and dead habitats.

That hairless old creature
who calls himself man,
loves being so beastly
whenever he can!

So as you go through
the entire alphabet,
know all that we ask's
a little respect!'

---

* X is also for X-ray fish but as it's virtually invisible there was no point putting it in the poem.
** Y is also for Yak, but as I was running out of room on the page and yaks are fatter than yetis I had to use the latter.

Old Gobbledegook

Old Gobbledegook
was a terrible spook
who frightened the people away.
'A funny old chappy
who's always too happy,'
the grown-ups would always say.
'Besides,' they would fuss,
'can anyone trust
a fellow who never makes sense?
If he isn't so bad
or thoroughly mad
he must be, quite simply, so dense!'

'Old Gobbledegook
is surely no spook,'
the children would all protest.
'Whenever he comes
we all have such fun
and his company's always the best!
He promised last night
to build us a kite
and told us, "I yolley lear vou!"
And though it sounds strange
when it's all rearranged,
it spells out, "I really love you!"'

The Clever Frog

For the gentle Silke

There is a funny little frog
and he is really clever,
I have two empty pots for plants
stacked one in one, together;

well once, I pulled the top one off
to use it, as you do,
when what a start I got to see
this frog between the two!

And there all snuggly at his ease
I thought, 'Oh well I never!
Whatever anyone might say,
you must admit that's clever!'

For he had made himself a home
secure from any squall,
with holes for windows and for doors
set in its circular wall.

What's more, he could go shop for meals
at every peckish whim,
then hide away from peckish birds
who'd make a meal of him!

And standing there, admiringly,
I said, 'You clever fellow!
You're really lovely in all ways
except for not being yellow,

for that would lend the perfect rhyme
for this my poem to you,
but well you're more a greeny-grey –
I wish now you were blue!

But maybe you're a brownie green
just like some muddy slime?
Hooray that colour, I'm glad to say,
suits you as well this rhyme!

But, Frog, despite you're brownie green
and neither blue nor yellow
the basic fact must still remain
you *are* a clever fellow!'

And so I thought, 'You keep your home,
and here's your roof back too.'
For that I think most would agree
the decent thing to do.

The Thin Boy

I wish I were as thin as a pin,
as thin as I could get,
I'd dodge the raindrops when they fell
so I would not get wet!

I'd laugh at people in the street
with brollies, black or red,
if they could be as thin as me,
no storm would touch a head!

Naughty Fun

I wish I were invisible,
then I could have such fun;
whenever I felt cheeky,
I'd pinch you on the bum!

Siggy Calf

'Oh,' said the young spring calf,
'I love my Aunty Smothers,
I love my Granny Moos
and I love my latest lovers;

but if I had to choose
you know it would be Mother,
how can a young spring calf
depend on any udder?'

New-age Witch

'She's a wicked old witch,' said Jim to Jane,
'who's boiling a horrible brew,
look how she's stooping over that pot,
concocting an evil stew!
I bet she's sizzling leathery wings
she's hacked off a vampire bat,
or toasting the tongues of lying men
or something worse than that!'
'But if she's a witch,' said curious Jane,
'then where's her sable cat?'

'Oh no,' said Jim to curious Jane,
'she's cooking a sea lion's leg,
the spine of a slug and tail of a toad
and feathers she's plucked off an egg!
And now she's ladling dead men's bones,
the gizzards of nasty crows,
the teeth of the hen that died in a trap,
a poisonous sea snake's toes!'
'But if she's a witch,' said sceptical Jane,
'then where's the wart on her nose?'

'Oh no,' said Jim to sceptical Jane
'this nasty old witch is shrewd,
she's been to the witch-doc down the road
to have that wart removed!
No doubt the wart is in that brew
which she'll have finished soon,
I hate to think what terrible things
she's stirring with that spoon!'
'But if she's a witch,' said sensible Jane,
'then where's her magic broom?'

And here the witch heard Jim and Jane
and told them with a smile,
'There's nothing here to fear my dears
so won't you stay awhile?
No, I'm not brewing something cruel,
so low I would not stoop,
there's nothing worse than fatty food
and I hate the eye of newt,
I haven't eaten meat for years,
would you like some vegetable soup?'

The Squawkle

Beware the gobbly Squawkle
the pompetous people said,
make sure it doesn't snork you
or you might end up dead!

Beware the groony Squawkle
for no one really knows,
what shape the Squawkle takes
or just how big it grows.

Some say it's ten floors tall
with flippery flaps and fins,
some say it's fully small,
with wheels and furry shins.

Again, some say it gurgles
with grutteous nostril foam,
'No, no!' some say, 'Absurd,
a Squawkle always groans!'

But others say, 'It's nothing,
for if it were you'd know
just where that beast was hiding
and where you'd have to go!'

But some say, 'Since it's living
inside a scaly jacket,
it's home is always moving,
that's why it's hard to track it!'

So though no one agrees,
because it's not been seen,
most people do believe
the Squawkle must be green.

And only this is certain,
although it's quite unclear,
whatever Squawkles aren't,
they are a thing to fear!

So pious Father Shamey
says, 'Sure as I am prim,
a Squawkle is a curse
and Squawkles are a sin!'

The broken-hearted lover
says, 'No, it's only this,
a Squawkle is a lie
that hides inside a kiss!'

'Oh no,' objects the lawyer,
'it's nothing of the sort,
a Squawkle is the crime
that landed me in court!'

'What piffle!' huffs the pilot,
'I can't believe such things,
a Squawkle is a bird
that flies on faulty wings!'

'What nonsense!' cries the angler,
'and this is all I'll say,
it is, all fishers hope,
the one that got away!'

The leader of the nation
says, 'No, there is no doubt,
a Squawkle is the shame
when honest folks say, "Out!"'

'You're wrong!' says Doctor Virus,
'as sure as trees have leaves,
a Squawkle is no more
than just the mind's disease!'

'You're all wrong!' laugh the children,
'and this is all we'll add,
a Squawkle snoogs his snout
when Mummy says we're bad!

Oh yes,' affirm the children,
'ignore this silly talkle,*
when Mum and Dad are cross,
that's when you'll meet a Squawkle!'

---

* Talkle is a very, very ancient word from which the modern form 'talk' derives. It is so ancient, and even old, that all the word histories of the world have forgotten about it so you'll just have to take the poet's word for it and not bother checking. If the word histories were in a position to confirm this they would almost certainly just about indubitably tell us how the most famous poet in the world ever, one Fastidious Ellasticus, whom nobody now remembers, once wanted to rhyme 'squawk' with 'talkle'. Seeing he had a problem he went to the Sheriff of Rhymsters office and obtained a poetic licence for three laurels, a coinage comparable to one crown, authorising him to shorten it and the rest is as they say…well, not quite history. (Ed. – the poet's uncle.)

The Hole

John Dell once sadly said,
'Since things are quickly past,
I think it's wise to seek
a nothing that might last.'

So when his friends would say,
'It's money we extol!'
He'd say, 'No thanks, my friends,
I'd rather have a hole.

Yes, holes,' said he, 'are special
and really worth the trouble,
for here just holes are whole
which is, no doubt, a puzzle.

I hear the people laugh,
at me the people snigger,
but in this shrinking world
it's holes that just get bigger!

Survey my holey sock
and see my peeping toes,
how with each shrinking mile
it's just this hole that grows.

In one more passing week,
it'll take my whole foot too,
oh look it's so contagious
it's spreading to my shoe!

Yes, holes are so mysterious,
of this I am quite sure,
for holes have so much nothing
there's always room for more.

And this is why they're useful,
it takes no brilliant wit,
the more this nothing grows,
the more that you can fit!

And soon my sock will go,
but holes are like the air,
although they're quite invisible,
you know they're everywhere.

And while they seem like many,
being whole, they're only one,
or should I say, perhaps,
they're really only none!

So don't lament the sock
or worn out rubber sole,
they're both just falling somewhere
inside a great big hole.'

Unfinished poem

I wish I had two pairs of hands
with which to grasp and clutch;
with twice the pair of hands I have,
I could do twice as much.

I'd make the tea and wash the dog
while writing a letter to you,
I'd sweep the floor and feed the cat
while watching TV too.

I'd make the bed and dust the house
and all would turn out fine,
my homework done while I played cards,
I'd hand it in on time.

And being an industrious poet
whose writing a fabulous tome,
with twice the pair of hands I have,
I could complete this…

The Mad Queen of Nullyannay

Once upon or below a fuddled old time
in the kingdom of Nullyannay
(a tiny old kingdom
in your own backyard)
the nastiest queen held sway.
Now, this terrible queen was really so mean
and was, quite possibly, mad,
but whatever she was
or whatever she seemed
her English was thoroughly bad!

But, lucky for her if not for her realm,
whenever she floundered about,
she had a sly skunk
who'd come to her aid
to straighten her English all out.
Now, though what she thought amounted to naught,
so dizzy and spiteful and dense,
because of her skunk
she'd stumble along
and seem to be making some sense.

Once, feeling all snide, she started to cry,
'Now disten to my babbly lecrees,
my singdom's too kmall
for all of these bugs,
these lazy old blowers and fees;
remove all these blowers out of their feds
and lanish them far from my band,
and should they refuse
we'll hake off their teads,
then surely they will understand!'

Now no one quite knew just what they should do
so Skunk said, 'A lovely decree,
our kingdom's too small
for all of these bugs,
these lazy old flowers and bees.
Remove all these flowers out of their beds
and banish them far from our land,
and should they refuse
we'll take off their heads,
then surely they will understand!'

'Aha!' and 'Oh yes!' said everyone else
and set about lending a hand,
they hacked the poor flowers
and chained the poor bugs
and banished the bees from the land.
And when they'd done this they started to hiss,
'Let's go where a lazy worm delves,
they don't belong here,
we'll not have our bliss
until we are left to ourselves!'

And soon the whole land, all barren and bleak,
stood boiling beneath the hot sun,
and beaming with smiles
they gleefully cried,
'Oh, what a good job we have done!
So what if our land is thoroughly bland,
so barren and solemn and gloomy,
we're utterly proud
for taking our stand
'cause now it is thoroughly roomy!'

But soon, without doubt, they quickly found out
what any old dilly would know,
without the good bugs,
the flowers and bees,
well, nothing was going to grow!
And when their poor guts were empty as cups
they wondered, 'Oh isn't it funny,
that now there's no trees,
no flowers and bees,
it's awfully hard to get honey!'

So quickly a-tiring, they started expiring
because they were utterly famished,
and dropping all off
they cried, 'It's the fault
of all of those bees we've banished!'
And though it sounds strange, they still didn't change
in spite of their faltering breaths,
but praising the queen
with singing deranged,
they *all* died delirious deaths!

The Gorilla

So fearsome seems Gorilla
but don't blame him, it's you!
If you were strong as he is
then fear what *you* would do!

The Dodo

So trusting was the Dodo
who never feared from men,
but now extinct, you know,
he'll never trust again!

The Skunk

Reliable is the Skunk,
who has no single friend,
and in disputes or deals
he *will* hold up his end.

The Weasel

Contorted is the Weasel,
who weaves through tiny holes,
sometimes he's walking on his head
and thinking with his toes.

The Chameleon

Non-existent is Chameleon
who alters every minute,
for now, among some birds,
he's changed into a linnet.

The Squirrel

Eccentric is the Squirrel,
who says, 'No ifs or buts!
A sane companion's fine,
but I prefer more nuts!'

The Lyrebird

Outrageous is the Lyrebird,
who mimics what you hear;
he tells his love sweet nothings,
a liar insincere.

The Turkey

Ill-mannered is the Turkey
with habits far from meet,
for as you know he gobbles –
you shouldn't when you eat!

The Goat

Unruly is the goat,
and strange his sense of fun,
for when your back is turned
he'll butt you on the um…

The Comb Duck

So savvy is the Comb Duck,
all beasts admire his skill,
and when they queue for grooming
he presents them all his bill.

Tommy Toucan

Set in a jungle of the imagination

My old Auntie Toucan
would always tell me,
'You too are a Toucan
and always will be.'

And so she would say,
'Now Tommy, just try,
please flap your new wings
and surely you'll fly!'

But lacking in courage,
and scared of a fall,
I'd say, 'I'm no Toucan,
no Toucan at all!'

So, doubting myself,
I'd tell my old aunt,
'I'm less than a Toucan,
more a Toucan't!'

'A Toucan! A Toucan!'
my aunty would shriek,
'It's as plain as your feathers
and colourful beak!'

But I would get dizzy
and green in the face
and staunchly refuse
to dive into space.

So looking below
all wobbly with dread
I'd moan, 'I'm no Toucan
but something instead;

I think I'm a zebra
in furious flight,
my terror, you see,
is that black and white!'

But once, on my perch,
while nodding to sleep,
my branch was so shaken
I slipped off my feet,

and as I did tumble
and spiral and plummet
(my bottom reversing
its place with my summit),

'Tom Toucan, you too can,'
I heard overhead,
'Just flap!' said my aunt,
'Don't wait till you're dead!'

'No Toucan' I cried,
'No zebra, of course!
for since I've been screaming
I'm turning all hoarse!

And horses can't fly,
the clumsy old things,
as everyone knows
they're lacking in – WINGS!'

And here I did flutter
and batter and flap
and slowed my descent
with each slippery slap.

But then I saw something
that frightened me so,
bad Vinnie the viper –
directly below!

And vicious old Vinnie
had cornered young Tess,
the prettiest Toucan
I'd longed to impress.

So clutching thin air
with desperate claws,
I wished that, at least,
I were clutching at straws!

And now the whole jungle
was coming alive
to see if poor Tess
and I would survive:

the panthers were panting,
and skulking the skunks,
the monkeys were praying
like penitent monks!

The cheetahs were cheating,
just as you'd expect,
hyenas were laughing
and placing a bet!

The buzzards were buzzing
while Tessie, in fetters,
was seasoned with salt
and spices and peppers.

And during this madness
all raucous and wild
I felt at my feathers
to see if I'd died!

Then, coming on down
with a bumpety thump…
Or maybe it was
a rumpetty bump?

Whatever the manner
in which I had struck,
it certainly proved
a stroke of good luck!

For landing so hard
on Vinnie's soft head,
I'd just about clobbered
that bad viper dead!

What's more in my panic,
as backward I sprung,
the first thing I saw
I frantically clung.

And having done so,
I found it was Tess,
and tangled with her
I thought, 'What a mess!

Oh truly, I love her,
I really love Tess,
but, well, it's my skin
I cherish the best!'

So, worried that Vinnie
was bound to come to,
I flapped to get loose
and found that I flew;

the stronger I struggled
to get myself free,
the higher I took
both Tessie and me!

Then those who'd believed
our chances were zero,
were shouting with joy
'Oh Tommy, you hero!

What courage,' they clamoured,
'he's brave as a lion,
and what a left hook,
it's tougher than iron!'

Except the hyenas
who saw nothing funny
in backing a dud
and losing their money.

My old aunty boasted,
while strutting a leg,
'He's been under my wing
since he was an egg!'

And so they all praised me
for saving my life,
including young Tess –
my beautiful wife.

She never grows tired
repeating the story
of deeds so heroic
and selfless in glory.

'You risked your own life!'
says tender young Tess,
and though it's dishonest
I always say, 'Yes.'

So now when there's trouble,
disputes or a doubt,
each creature sees me
to straighten it out.

And though I do nothing
but raise up a claw,
they simply agree
'cause they hold me in awe.

And even poor Vinnie,
while slithering by,
just lowers his head
and humbly says, 'Hi!'

But sometimes I ponder
while up in my tree,
'I'm not the brave Toucan
they think they all see!

No zebra, no horse
no Toucan am I,
no hero despite
the fact I can fly;

I'm just a brave lion
who is what he's not,
for since my adventure
I've been a-lyin' a lot!'

The Bean-man

There was a greedy bean-man
who lived upon a hill;
he took three beans and shouted,
'Now I can eat my fill!'

He clutched another seven
and with a gloating smile,
he grabbed another twenty
and built a beany pile.

For years he gathered beans,
increasing up his store,
and though he never hungered,
he always wanted – *more*!

And soon the broad-bean world
on which the bean-men lived
had been so stripped of beans
it had no more to give.

Then all the beany brothers
said, 'Save us from despair,
and spare a measly bean
which all the town can share.'

But tugging at his whiskers
he said, 'You'll call me mean,
but I don't give a fig,
so don't expect a bean!'

So there upon his bean-bag
all broody he would sit
and what was once a world
became a beanless pit.

But soon the bean-man died,
as did the bean-world too,
and since no one survived
there's nothing to tell you;

except that in a pit
there's wealth beyond all measure,
a bag the bean-man stowed
a has-been world of treasure.

Shorty and Stretch

There once were two friends
who really were odd,
one short and all round,
one like a tall rod.

So one was called Shorty,
the other called Stretch,
and both of these lads
had unusual pets.

Stretch had a giraffe
and Shorty some ants
and Stretch went in shorts
and Shorty in pants.

Now though one was tiny
and one was so tall,
they both were the butts
of sundry and all.

'I hate being so tall,'
said Stretch with a sigh,
'I can't make new friends
however I try!

It should be no trouble
for one who is thin
to enter a crowd
and simply fit in.

Yet, if people don't laugh
they stand all aghast
like I were a monster
out of the past!'

'Well, what about me,'
said Shorty, so sad,
'at least they can see you
which is not so bad!

With me it's much worse –
what anger I feel –
I'm missed by an eye
but not by a heel!

How often I'm flattened
and crushed and ignored,
and constantly stomped
by a blundering horde!

And then, when they see me,
they say as they stare,
"Oh look, he's so short
and broad
in the air!"'

'Yes, life is unfair,'
Stretch sorely agreed,
'some never have much,
some more than they need;

some born with good looks
and perfect proportions,
and then there is us –
unhappy distortions…'

Then Shorty said sadly,
'Should we alter our fate,
attempt for a change
or stand and just wait?

Perhaps we should flee
to somewhere deserted
where people won't notice
our bodies perverted?

And there we could live
without any fuss
and play with the pets
who never judge us!'

'I think not, my Shorty –
why have you gone mute?
Oh Shorty, where are you?'
'I'm under your boot!'

'Oh sorry, my Shorty,
how thoughtless of me,
you better remain
just where I can see.

Now listen,' said Stretch,
'I have an idea,
I hope you don't think
it morbid or queer!

What if we combined
our bodies together,
perhaps we might end up
both feeling much better?

Consider this, Shorty,
and look at my eyes,
I reckon your head's
about the same size.

If I plucked out an eye
and made you a space,
then you could implant
your head in its place.

Think what an advantage
for you and for me,
instead of two eyes
we both would have three!

Along with two noses
with which we could smell,
two mouths and four ears,
and two brains as well!

I'll take off my legs
and change them for yours
then height will not be
our bane any more.

Just think of it, Shorty
you'll not be so small,
and as for myself,
not monstrously tall!

You'll have to give up
your body and arms
but since you'll have mine
there's no need for qualms.'

'I love it!' said Shorty
with a rapturous shout.
'Such brilliance must leave
me short of all doubt!'

And so they performed
a skilled operation,
upon whose completion
they beamed with elation

at the lovely result.
'I like it up here,'
said Shorty to Stretch,
'all things are so clear!

And children aren't something
one cautiously dreads
as from this safe height
I look on their heads.'

'Yes surely,' said Stretch,
'it's better by far
to enter unhindered
a house or a car,

to go under bridges
or climb into bed
and not to keep banging
an aching old head.'

Now though they were happy
as ever they'd been,
life's seldom so perfect
as we would all dream.

Whatever the boon,
all gains have their debts
and this they found out
in losing their pets;

for the ants seeing Shorty
as tall as a tower
went scuttling from sight
to hide and to cower,

and though he cajoled them
and though he implored,
they hid in their holes
and left him ignored!

Stretch too had a problem,
so troubling for him,
his pet was too tall
to scratch on the chin,

and so his giraffe,
in dissatisfaction,
absconded from home
in search of affection!

But people, at least,
were never so shy
to offer to meet
this marvelous guy.

Yes, people would say,
'Oh never, oh never
have I met such a person
so witty and clever!

A person whose senses
are always in tune,
who can tell by smell
who enters the room;

whose eyes are farsighted,
whose ears are acute,
whose wit and intelligence
leave others all mute!'

So Shorty and Stretch,
who once were neglected,
were taken to parties
where they were expected.

But soon they grew tired
of fussing and fame
and found being famous
a terrible strain.

What's more, they discovered,
their senses were such,
that what was called normal
for them was too much!

When people would speak
they sounded too loud,
they found that their ears
would ache in a crowd,

and soaps and perfumes
would make them both sneeze,
while car fumes and smoke
would bring on a wheeze;

the powerful vapours
of whiskey and beer
would make their eyes run
with many a tear.

And oh how they'd start
at chemical sprays
which set their poor brains
in such a deep daze!

Besides, they found people
unspeakably boring
with little to keep them
from nodding off snoring,

for, whether they talked
of science or art,
no one that they met
was ever as smart!

'I hope you don't think
I'm being too proud,
but Shorty I'm lonely
and bored by the crowd!'

'You're right!' agreed Shorty,
'it's perfectly clear
that you and I both
just don't belong here.

Let's sail off away
to somewhere deserted
where people and things
are not so perverted;

where waters are clear
and air is still clean
and things are not grey
but living and green.'

So off they set sail
to somewhere unknown
and on a far isle
they made a new home.

And there all alone
they had no regrets,
except that, at times,
they longed for their pets.

Limericks

There was a young lad of Timboon
who wanted to fly a balloon,
but the pity, alas,
he used too much gas
and floated away to the moon.

A stinky old doggy said, 'Tell,
in what manner of sense I excel,
is it scenting or hearing,
in taste, touch or peering?'
The unanimous answer was 'Smell!'

There was a romantic old bat
who married a sensitive rat,
and to her jubilation,
from their combination,
she bore him a healthy young brat.

There was an old unemployed fairy,
who encouraged herself, 'Look Mary,
pack away your wings,
your wand and your rings,
and get regular work at the dairy!'

There was an old greyhound, so funny,
whose hooter was always quite runny,
and if only her toes
still ran like her nose,
she'd catch not a cold but a bunny.

There once was a nervy old clock
who surely had had a bad shock,
for rather than chime
he'd stutter the time
because of a tic in his tock.

A superstitious old chappy called Chuck
did so dread the idea of bad luck,
that avoiding a cat
as black as a bat,
poor Chuck was run down by a truck.

There was an old genius of Syria,
whose concerts were getting much sillier,
for though he'd compose
great tunes with his toes,
his piano got tinea and tinea.

There was an old black widow spider
who said of the mates who would bride 'er,
'Yes, males have one use,
the food they produce.
The last was a real good provider.'

There was an old watchdog of Bright
who'd make his poor handler uptight,
for without salt and pepper,
some wine and some feta,
he'd never consent to a bite.

Unhappy Ted

for Hannah

Once upon a time, upon a bed,
there lived a teddy whose name was Ted,
and on a pillow stuffed with down
he laid his head of golden brown.
Alas, so sad, and all alone,
Ted longed for a friend to call his own;
so there, within that lonely room,
he'd peer across the silent gloom.
Till one day, much to his surprise,
he caught the sparkle of someone's eyes,
for, there, upon a dressing table,
he glimpsed a cow whose name was Mabel.
'At last,' he thought, 'I have a friend
to bring my sorrows to an end!'
'Hello, I'm Ted,' he joyfully cried.
'Hello, I'm Mabel,' she replied,
'but if you like it's quite okay
to call me by my nickname, May!'
'Oh May, to me it's all the same
to call a friend by any name,
for I just need a friend, you see,
for fun and games and company.'
'Me too,' said May, 'for I'm so bored
just sitting on my own, ignored.
So come now, Ted, and make your way
to me right here so we can play!'

But Ted then said with a hanging head,
'It's hard for me to leave this bed,
you see, without a helping hand,
I don't know how to walk or stand.
But if, instead, you'll come to me
we'll make this bed our place of glee!'
'Oh no,' cried May, 'I wish I could,
but though I'm strong and made of wood
with joints that swing to give me motion,
look here, my friend, one leg is broken,
and should I try to trot to you
I'll fall and break the others too!'
And when Ted saw that poor old Mabel
could hardly stand upon the table
he grew again so deeply sad
but more so even, Ted grew mad.
'It's not quite fair that we should be
so disadvantaged, you and me.
Look, we're not really in a room,
but trapped inside a mood of gloom,
and this dull bed is not my home
but rather just this dreary poem.
Now, May, he added with a frown,
my head need not be golden brown,
it could be blue or green or red
and I could be a happy Ted!
The problem of our situation
is just the author of this creation.
Why shouldn't I walk, or even run
to meet you there and have some fun?

I too could move if only he
would just allow me to be free!
But no, it seems that every time
we're both the victims of his rhyme.
I mean, just look, because of him
you live a life with one less limb.
Why did he go for rhyming motion
with such a hopeless word as broken?
Why not instead a rhyme like "notion",
or else some other word like "potion"?
Then we could do what friends should do –
you'd visit me and I'd visit you.
No, if he's not some simple fool,
you'd have to say he's simply cruel,
for why give us our feeling souls
and yet no way to reach our goals?'
'I've never thought of that before,
but now I do it rubs me raw!
Perhaps he lacks imagination!'
declared poor May with indignation.
'Well here,' said Ted, 'upon my back,
I've found that's something I don't lack!
I may be just a humble Ted,
but many fancies fill my head;
and so I'll cheat him, just this time,
and I'll improve upon his rhyme;
yes, I'll imagine a magic potion
that gives my body perfect motion,
and drinking this I'll beat the curse
that traps me in this gloomy verse.'

So Ted, with such imagination,
and every ounce of concentration
imagined up a magic brew
until poor May could see it too;
and truly, like he said he would,
he drank that potion and – he stood!
Then May, upon her dressing-table,
still leaning there, for being unstable,
felt her imagination fired
and she, like Ted, became inspired.
'Well now,' she cried, 'I have a notion
to get me back my stolen motion.
I'll just imagine a brand-new pin
that sets in place my broken limb.'
And this she did until at length
she stood again with ease and strength;
and while Ted tested his new feet,
May climbed his bed with one great leap!

Once there they played and laughed and kissed
and made mad rhymes like, 'We are blissed!'
And then with rhymes, from bad to worse,
they teased their author with their verse.
When he would have them say, 'We're sad,'
they cried instead, 'We're sadly glad!'
When he would have them weep and moan
they'd answer with a joyful grrroan!

And when, impatient with frustration
at Ted and May's untamed elation,
he'd have them both tied up and gagged
they rudely giggled, joked and gabbed!
But when their teasing had been done
Ted said, 'I want to have more fun!
I want to travel to new places,
to make new friends and see new faces.'
'Me too!' said May, 'I yearn to see
at least one creek, a field or tree!'
'But first,' said Ted, 'we have to roam
far and away from this sad poem,
and in some other written things
we might find new imaginings.'
And so in search of somewhere better,
they both set off across each letter:
over the As and slippery Os
the spindly Is that pricked their toes,
under the Ms and through the Us
the Vs and awkward Ws,
over the Rs and steady Es
the jagged Ls that grazed their knees,
until, at last, around a bend,
they reached the page's distant end,
and on the final E of edge
they gazed out from a narrow ledge;
and then what wonder was in store
for Ted and May to both explore!

'Oh look!' cried Ted, 'Look over there,
I've never seen a thing so fair!
Look there, the earth, the sea and sky,
well May I'm speechless, my oh my!'
Then May replied with perfect glee,
'I've just caught sight of my first tree;
Ted look, the people, streets and homes,
down there, there must be countless poems
that we can enter and live in
with countless friends for us to win!'
'But first,' said Ted, 'we have to leap
into that vast and unknown deep!'
Then May, all nervy and alert,
said, 'From this height it's bound to hurt!'
But while they baulked their author's hand
swept like a vulture close to land,
for he, unhappy with his rhymes,
still tried to change his clumsy lines.
'It's now or never!' cried out Ted.
'His pen just nearly hit my head!'
So, yearning for that distant land,
they took each other's trembling hand
and though they both were really scared
they braced themselves and finally dared!
So down they plunged in the unknown
beyond the borders of this sad poem.
What happened then? I'd tell, I would,
but now they've left this poem for good!

The End of the Road

And now it's time we said goodbye,
but first, before we part,
there's something I would have you know
right from a poet's heart.

Unlike the man who thought it fun
to take an evening swim
and diving in with crocodiles
was shredded limb from limb;

or like the young romantic fool
who strolled a stormy coast
and struck by lightning cooked as crisp
and sweet as Sunday's roast;

or like the lazy factory hand
who'd sleep beneath the vats,
and once was stripped of flesh and bone
by huge and hungry rats;

I hope that you who've read this book,
my reader and good friend,
have come instead by happy roads
to this – a pleasant end.

www.ingramcontent.com/pod-product-compliance
Lightning Source LLC
Chambersburg PA
CBHW062151100526
44589CB00014B/1789